What Kind of Animal Is It?

Animals Called Mammals

Bobbie Kalman & Kristina Lundblad

A Crabtree Crown Book

Crabtree Publishing

crabtreebooks.com

Animals Called Mammals

Editor-in-chief
Bobbie Kalman

Writing team
Bobbie Kalman
Kristina Lundblad

Substantive editor
Kathryn Smithyman

Editors
Molly Aloian
Robin Johnson
Kelley MacAulay
Reagan Miller

Design
Samara Parent

Consultant
Patricia Loesche, Ph.D., Animal Behavior Program, Department of Psychology, University of Washington

Production manager
Candice Campbell

Photographs Shutterstock; p23: Danny Ye/Shutterstock

Illustrations Barbara Bedell : page 6

Crabtree Publishing

crabtreebooks.com 800-387-7650

In Canada: We acknowledge the financial support of the Government of Canada through the Canada Book Fund for our publishing activities.

Printed in the U.S.A./CP032026

Published in Canada
Crabtree Publishing
616 Welland Ave.
St. Catharines,
Ontario L2M 5V6

Published in the United States
Crabtree Publishing
347 Fifth Ave.
Suite 1402-145
New York, NY 10016

Hardcover: 978-1-0398-7314-8
Paperback: 978-1-0398-7372-8
Ebook (pdf): 978-1-0398-7421-3
Epub: 978-1-0398-7470-1

Library and Archives Canada Cataloguing in Publication
Available at Library and Archives Canada

Library of Congress Cataloging-in-Publication Data
Available at the Library of Congress

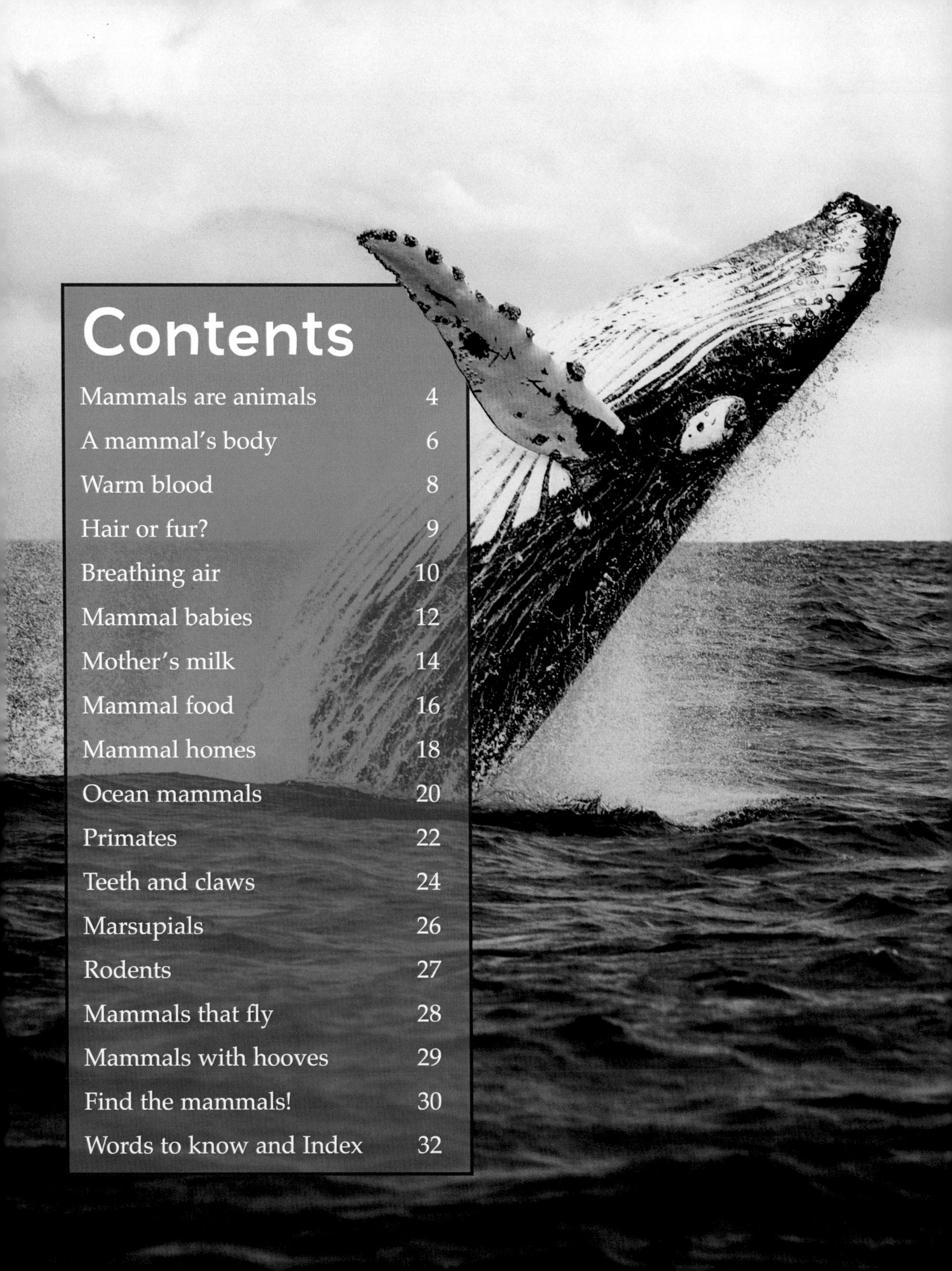

Contents

Mammals are animals

Mammals are animals. There are different kinds of mammals. Each kind belongs to a group. Some mammal groups are shown on these pages.

*Horses are mammals that have **hooves** (see page 29).*

Elephants make up their own group of mammals.

Bats are mammals that can fly (see page 28).

Gerbils are mammals that have long front teeth (see page 27).

Lions are mammals that have sharp teeth for tearing meat (see page 24).

Platypuses are mammals that lay eggs (see page 13).

Gorillas are mammals that have hands (see pages 22–23).

Koalas are mammals that have pouches for holding their babies (see page 26).

Whales are mammals that live in water (see pages 20–21).

A mammal's body

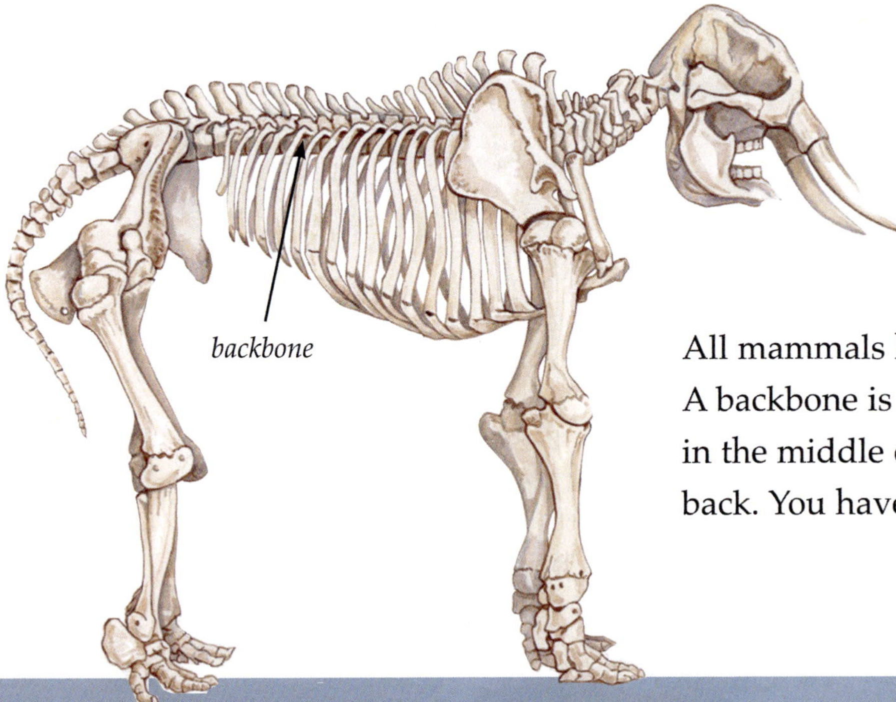

All mammals have **backbones**. A backbone is a group of bones in the middle of an animal's back. You have a backbone, too!

Elephants have backbones.

Mammals have limbs

Mammals have **limbs**. A limb can be an arm, a leg, a flipper, or a wing. Some mammals use their limbs to hold things. Mammals also use their limbs to move around. Different mammals move around in different ways. Many mammals walk and run. Some mammals hop, and others swim or fly.

This baby bear is using its front legs to move a piece of wood.

This clouded leopard uses its four legs to walk, run, and climb.

Warm blood

The body temperature of a fox is about the same in summer as it is in winter.

All mammals are **warm-blooded**. The body temperatures of warm-blooded animals always stay about the same. It does not matter if the animals are in cold places or warm places. Take your temperature a few times during a day. Your temperature should always be about the same because you are warm-blooded.

Even in very cold weather, a fox's body temperature does not change.

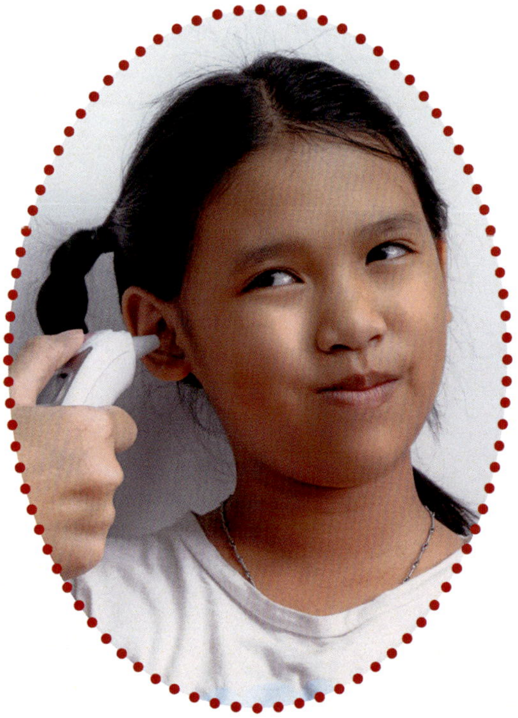

Your body temperature should be about 98.6° F (37° C). If your temperature changes very much, it could mean that you are sick.

Hair or fur?

Most mammals have hair or fur on their bodies. Some mammals have thick fur that keeps them warm and dry. Others have thin hair. People have hair. Human hair can be straight or curly.

Dogs and cats have fur on their bodies.

Rabbits have fur on their bodies. Some have long fur, and others have short fur.

Sheep are covered in ***wool****. Wool is a soft, curly kind of hair.*

Breathing air

Mammals need to breathe **oxygen** to stay alive. Oxygen is the part of air they need. They use their **lungs** to breathe air. Lungs are body parts that take in air. Lungs also let out air.

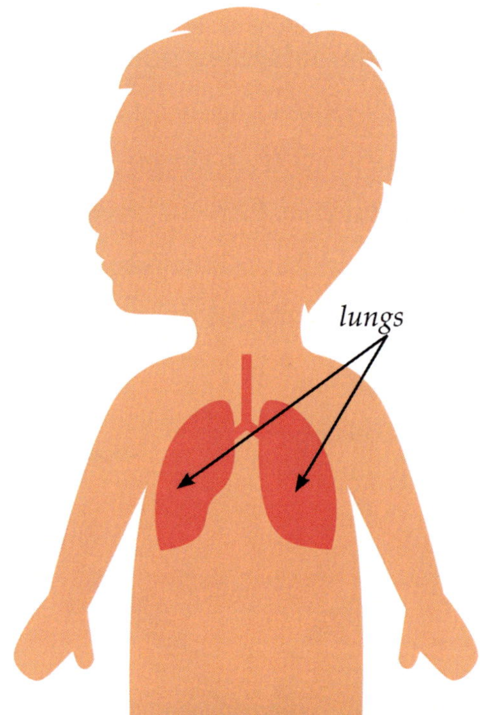

Breathe in, breathe out

When you breathe in, you take in air through your nose or mouth and into your lungs. When you breathe out, your lungs push out air through your nose or mouth. The girl shown left is blowing bubbles. The air in the bubbles came from her lungs.

Coming up for air

Fish can take in oxygen from water, but mammals cannot. Mammals that live in water must swim to the surface of the water to breathe air. Dolphins are mammals that live in water. They breathe air through **blowholes**. A blowhole is a hole on the top of a dolphin's head.

A dolphin opens its blowhole to breathe in. A dolphin closes its blowhole when it goes under water.

The dolphin's blowhole is closed.

The dolphin's blowhole is open.

A baby gorilla is born live.

Mammal babies

Most mammal babies grow inside the bodies of their mothers. Some female mammals carry their babies inside their bodies for only a few weeks. Others carry their babies for more than a year. Mammal babies are **born live**. Animals that are born live do not hatch from eggs the way birds do.

Some mammals have only one baby at a time. Other mammals have ***litters****. A litter is a group of babies born at the same time. How many baby lions are in this litter?*

Mammal eggs

Most baby mammals are born live, but baby platypuses are not. Baby platypuses hatch from eggs. The eggs are laid by their mothers. A female platypus lays between one and three eggs at a time.

Caring for babies

Most mammal mothers care for their babies after the babies are born. Some baby mammals stay with their mothers or with both parents for a long time. Other baby mammals leave their mothers after a few months to live on their own.

*Baby deer are called **fawns**. Some fawns stay with their mothers for up to two years.*

Mother's milk

Mammal babies drink milk soon after they are born. They are the only animal babies that drink milk. The milk they drink comes from the bodies of their mothers. Drinking mother's milk is called **nursing**. As baby mammals grow, they nurse less often. Eventually, they begin eating the same foods as the food their parents eat.

This monk seal mother has only one baby that is nursing. The leopard mother on the right has two babies that are nursing at the same time.

Mammal food

After mammals stop nursing, they need to find their own food. They need food so they can grow and stay healthy. Different mammals eat different foods. Some mammals eat only plants. Plant-eating animals are called **herbivores**. Herbivores eat bark, grass, leaves, seeds, and flowers. Elephants, deer, and rabbits are herbivores.

Rabbits eat grass and other plants that grow close to the ground.

Food for mammals

Some mammals are **carnivores**. Carnivores are animals that eat other animals. Cats, wolves, and ferrets are carnivores. Some mammals eat both plants and animals. These animals are called **omnivores**. Raccoons, bears, and foxes are omnivores.

Ferrets are carnivores. They eat rabbits, frogs, birds, and lizards.

Foxes are omnivores. They eat frogs, mice, and birds, but they also eat many kinds of plants.

Mammal homes

Mammals live all over the world. They live in many kinds of **habitats**. A habitat is the natural place where an animal lives. Most mammals live on land. Forests, mountains, and deserts are land habitats. A few types of mammals live in water. Oceans, lakes, and rivers are water habitats.

*Zebras live in areas that are covered in grasses. This kind of habitat is called a **grassland**.*

Wolverines live in forests.

Mountain goats live on mountains.

Polar bears live in a cold habitat called the Arctic. This habitat is covered in ice and snow for most of the year.

Ocean mammals

Some mammals live in oceans. Manatees, whales, and dolphins live their whole lives in water. Sea lions, seals, and walruses live on land and in water. They have their babies on land, but they look for food in oceans.

Orcas are the biggest dolphins. They spend all their time in the ocean. Orcas hunt seals and other dolphins for food.

Manatees can stay under water for up to 20 minutes. They then have to come up for air!

Staying warm

Most mammals that live in oceans have thick layers of **blubber** under their skin. Blubber is fat. Blubber helps keep mammals that live in oceans warm. Other ocean mammals have thick fur.

Sea otters do not have blubber. Their thick fur coats help keep their bodies warm.

Harp seals have blubber. Baby harp seals also have fluffy fur. They lose their fur a few weeks after they are born.

Primates

Monkeys, apes, lemurs, and humans belong to a group of mammals called **primates**. Some primates are big. Gorillas are big. Other primates are small. The bush baby on the left is small.

a gorilla's hand

Hang on!

Primates are the only mammals that have hands. Each hand has four fingers and one thumb. Primates use their hands to pick up objects. They also use their hands to hold on to branches.

Japanese snow monkeys live in families, as do many other primates. Family members care for one another.

People and spider monkeys are both primates. This woman is studying spider monkeys to find out more about them.

The smartest mammals

Primates are smart animals! They have large brains that help them learn quickly. Some primates use tools to help them find food and do other jobs.

A chimpanzee eats leaves, fruits, nuts, and insects. It uses a stick to find insects.

Teeth and claws

Some mammals have bodies that are built for hunting and for eating other animals. These mammals have sharp teeth and long, pointed claws. Cats, dogs, foxes, and bears have teeth and claws for hunting.

Polar bears have long, pointed claws.

Big cats, such as this tiger, use their sharp teeth to bite other animals. Lions and leopards are other big cats.

Wolves and pet dogs

Wolves are related to pet dogs. Wolves hunt for food together in groups called **packs**. Pet dogs live with people. People feed and care for the dogs.

This German shepherd is a pet dog. It looks a lot like the wolves in the picture above.

Marsupials

Koalas, kangaroos, and opossums belong to a group of mammals called **marsupials**. Most female marsupials have pouches on their bodies.

Baby inside!

When a baby marsupial is born, it is tiny and weak. It stays inside its mother's pouch until it has finished growing. It drinks milk inside the pouch. After a few months, the baby is strong enough to leave the pouch.

A baby kangaroo is called a ***joey****. This joey is big enough to leave its mother's pouch, but it crawls back into the pouch when it is scared or hungry.*

Rodents

Rodents are mammals with long, sharp front teeth. Their front teeth never stop growing! Rodents bite hard things to make sure their teeth do not grow too long. Biting hard things also keeps rodent teeth sharp. Most rodents have sharp claws, too.

The capybara is the largest rodent. It can weigh over 100 pounds (45 kg)!

Groundhogs are rodents. They live in grassy fields and forests.

Prairie dogs are rodents. Prairie dogs are called "dogs" because they sometimes make barking noises.

Mammals that fly

Bats are the only mammals with wings. They use their wings to fly. Bats cannot **glide** the way birds can. To glide is to float in air. Bats must keep flapping their wings to stay in the air.

Bat food

Most bats eat insects, but a few kinds of bats eat fish, mice, and birds. Some bats eat fruit.

Bats hang upside down while they rest. Many bats rest during the day and find food at night.

Mammals with hooves

Some mammals have hooves. Hooves are hard coverings that protect a mammal's feet. Hooves are sometimes divided into parts. Camel hooves have two parts. Rhinoceros hooves have three parts. Horse hooves are not divided into parts.

A camel's hooves have two parts.

A horse's hooves are not divided into parts.

A rhinoceros has hooves that are divided into three parts.

Find the mammals!

Mammals are all around you! Your pet may be a mammal. Many mammals live right in your back yard! Look at the pictures on these pages. Which of these animals are mammals? Which are not mammals?

Name all the mammals that people have as pets. How many mammals did you name?

Remember:

- most mammals have hair or fur on their bodies
- mammals have warm blood
- mammal babies drink milk
- some mammals live on land, and others live in water
- mammals breathe air

Are birds mammals? Birds are not mammals. Birds do not have hair or fur. They have feathers.

Is a ferret a mammal? Yes, it is a mammal. When it was a baby, it drank milk from its mother's body.

Is a fish a mammal? No, it is not a mammal. Fish are not warm-blooded animals.

Is a lizard a mammal? No, it is not a mammal. Baby lizards do not drink milk from the bodies of their mothers.

Is a raccoon a mammal? Yes, it is a mammal. A raccoon breathes air.

Words to know and Index

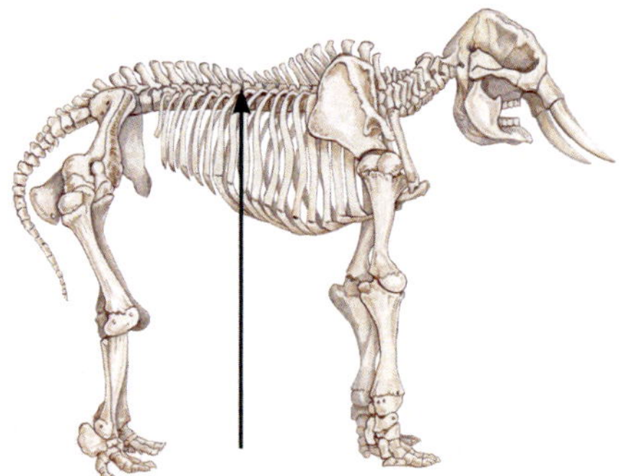

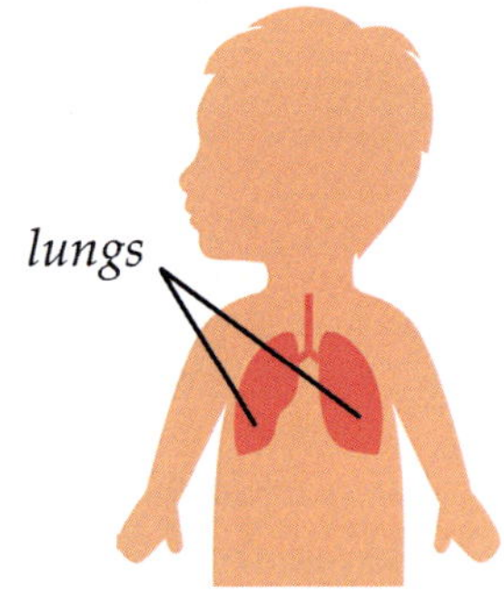